First Ladies
Voice

Pastor Lorraine Jenkins-Wilkes
(First Lady)
Inspired by True Events

First Ladies Voice

Copyright © 2020 by Pastor Lorraine Jenkins-Wilkes.
ISBN: 978-1-7346393-3-9

All rights reserved. No part of this book may be reproduced or transmitted in any form or by any means, electronic or mechanical, including photocopying, recording, or by any information storage and retrieval system, without permission in writing from the copyright owner.

This book was printed in the United States of America.

FOREWORD

Pastor Lorraine Jenkins-Wilkes is a woman who speaks with transparency and reveals the entire truth on life situations. Her revelations are not sugar-coated but are 100% pure and raw, such as is written in this book, First Ladies Voice.

For so long, First Ladies have had to play the theatrical roles like those in a Grammy Award-winning show. They learn their parts and they play them well, which is the role of being the loyal and dedicated wife to their husbands at all cost. Often, this meant they would suffer humiliation, ridicule, degradation, and embarrassment. Even so, they always kept those beautiful, painted smiles on their faces.

This book will reveal some of those naked truths that women married to pastors endure. Many of the stories are sad when the abuse, infidelity, and outside children by other female parishioners are depicted. Nevertheless, it is time that it is known that "everything that glitters is not gold." Behind those beautiful made-up faces, and those name brand suits, and those red-bottomed stilettos, are some very miserable, unhappy, and neglected ladies who deserve much better than they receive.

Read as she shares some of these truths, and then think about it. Is this what being a First Lady of a Church is all about, and if not, what should it be? As you read this book written by Pastor Lorraine Jenkins-Wilkes, these truths are revealed to you.

> Bishop Brenda Gale Peace
> Pastor of Greater Zion United Church
> Henderson, NC

First Ladies Voice

In honor of every pastor's wife struggling to use their voice.

Thank you for the special gift God has given you to endure as good soldiers.

"For his anger lasts only a moment, but his favor lasts a lifetime; weeping may endure for the night, but rejoicing comes in the morning." (Psalm 30:5 NIV)

I know it is hard to speak up sometimes. There is a time to be quiet and a time to speak. God will give you the right moment to say what is in your heart. You are the Queen of the Church where God has placed you. Do not be afraid.

"For the Spirit of God does not make us timid, but gives us power, love and self-discipline." (2 Timothy 1:7 NIV)

We are powerful, mighty and strong.

I honor you for your tenacity to push and do what God called you to do.

To my Lord and Savior, Jesus Christ:

Thank you for placing this burden on my heart.
Lord, I thank you for power and strength. I thank you for the authoritative voice on the inside of me, the Holy Ghost leading and guiding me. I pray that as people read these short stories, they will have compassion for each other.

~ TO THE READERS ~

Once again thank you for your support. You have been with me through Forever Home, Courage to Change and Courage to Change Devotional.
Remember, you have the power to do whatever God has commissioned you to do.
Domestic violence of any sort is not acceptable.
Speak up. Disrespect is not love.

"I praise you because I am fearfully and wonderfully made; your works are wonderful, I know that full well. (Psalms 139:14 NIV)

If you are affiliated with a church, pray for the pastor's wife. You have no idea what she may have to endure before she touches the church doors. Pray for each other without ceasing.

God bless you for your support.

Lorraine

ACKNOWLEDGEMENTS

My husband, Donnie Ray Wilkes
Son Jeffrey Dont'e McKelvin
Margie Urbina Mckelvin
Bonus Children: Timothy Wilkes
Sherice Wilkes
Carla Wilkes

Editor: Jessica Stone

CONTENTS

Introduction 15

Story 1 The Fragrance 19

Story 2 Unfilled 31

Story 3 Betrayal 43

Story 4 The Perfect Couple 52

Story 5 My Marriage Mate 58

Story 6 Dating while married 65

Story 7 District Lady Samantha 70

INTRODUCTION

Often when we hear someone speak of a "First Lady," we think of the First Lady married to the President of the United States of America. This First Lady lives at the White House. We think about the vital role she plays as the wife of the most important man in America. This title came into use in the 1800s. The phrase is used when the person in question is either the wife or female equivalent of a well-known person. This great woman is spoken about more than the President at times. She is loved and hated depending on what charities she has a passion for and how well she dresses.

This book is not about the First Lady of the United States of America, as high as she is. I am writing about the controversial title given to the First Lady, Queen of the black Christian Church. The black faith communities have given the distinct unofficial title of First Lady to the pastor's wife in the church. This title lets everyone in the church know that she is the number one lady in the church, married to the pastor. The shame at times is that there is a number two (or more) with whom she competes.

The title First Lady has caused some women in the church to become jealous and dislike the pastor's wife. The women say, "If she is the First Lady, who are we?" If she is first, who is the second, third, or fourth lady? The 'First Lady' title has caused some women to pursue the pastor to become the First Lady by any means necessary. I heard one member of a church stand up and say: "I love the pastor, and I am going to be the First Lady of this Church." It seems like this title causes more controversy than help in the church.

I am not sure how or when we started using this title. The First Lady's position or name is not biblically based. Where did her appointment originate? There is no mention of her in the Bible.

There are no instructions in God's word on conferring the title "First Lady" on anyone; there is no office or role of "First Lady" in the local church. In (Ephesians 4:11-13 NIV), Paul lists the various offices that were established by Christ for the church's attainment of the whole measure of the fullness of Christ. Not once is the office, role, or title of First Lady ever mentioned. The passage does not say 'a pastor's wife.' Those offices that are listed – apostle, prophet, evangelist, pastor, and teacher – are not titles, but offices or functions.

The title of First Lady is a tradition of addressing the pastor's wife in an honorable way. This distinction comes from the secular practice of giving unique distinction and honor to the wives of national chiefs or heads of state (presidents, prime ministers, governors, etc.). The reasoning is, since recognition goes to the office of the President of the United States, for example, then honor should also be given to his spouse. Thus, First Lady Michelle Obama or First Lady Laura Bush. This reasoning extended to the church setting as well since pastors are doing a mightier work for God himself than any earthly head of state.

Surely, they (and their wives) deserve at least as much honor. The thought seems to be, what's right for the President and First Lady of the White House is suitable for the Pastor and "First Lady" of God's house.

Introduction

In many churches, the "First Lady" is often deemed a leader herself, with decision-making authority in every facet of the ministry. By mere virtue of who she is married to, she is allowed to have an almost equal say in everything that goes on in the department. However, this is not true in every church. There are some churches where it is quite the opposite; she has no say in running the church, and is treated with disrespect. Some of them do not allow poor treatment of themselves – some places treat her like a queen.

This book is based on the voices of seven ladies who married pastors. These gifted women married pastors for their different reasons. We will read about the uniqueness of these women and the account of their experiences. The stories are based on real-life experiences, although none of the characters are real.

These ladies dreamed of marrying men who would make a difference in the world. Some wanted a powerful man. Others just wanted a husband. Some only wanted to sleep with the pastor for pure sexual pleasure. They thought when they married the Pastor of the Church, automatically, a good life was to happen. They have the experience of joy with their servant husband. Most wanted to serve God, and please the people of God.

These ladies were in for the biggest challenges of their lives. They are to discover pain and joy as never before. They will learn to lay before the Lord to pray and fight for the right to use their voices. They believed that they married into a saintly world, where everyone was loved. They soon discover some ugly truths. They will have to be keen to survive the world of the saints.

Seven different holy women called the First Lady, and some churches have recently in the year of 2017 taken off the 'First' and address some Pastor's wives as 'Lady' with their name, (for example, Lady Jones). The accounts of their stories and what happened to them hopefully will give us a better perspective on these special women in the church. Get ready for the journey.

STORY NUMBER ONE
The Fragrance

With a fragrance of royalty, First Lady Naomi walked into the sanctuary, like a Queen. The scent of her fragrant perfume fills the sanctuary like flowers ready to bloom as she sashays across the temple. Her attire demands notice as everyone turns around, paying attention to her. They should be giving full attention to Pastor Michaels, who was ready to preach to his people.

First Lady Naomi, a gorgeous five feet nine inches in height, is comfortable with eyes on her as she walks into the church. She gives the show they are looking for, wearing a big wide-brim white hat with blinding rhinestones. Her coral Saint John knit suit definitely fit her shapely, ample body like it was made just for her.

On her lovely long legs, she wore pantyhose that cost her one hundred dollars a pair. The women in the church examined her from head to toe, searching for something out of place. A hair, run in stockings, string hanging, or maybe slip lines showing. It took her three hours to get dressed. Naomi made sure there was nothing out of place in her appearance. The Sisters in the church examined her from the top of her head to her feet. Their eyes roll down to the two thousand-dollar, four-inch red bottom shoes giving extra height to her already tall frame. The match of her hat sets off the outfit. Her scarf was in her right hand, held delicately as if it were a feather. The beautiful silver tailor-made silk scarf was embroidered with her monogrammed initials. She was flawless, and the woman who did not like her, with all their usual critiques, find nothing that day to gossip about. Her large brim hat covers most of her face. Her make up is immaculate, not overdone. Her lips are a glossy pink color.

Pastor Michaels frowns, growing weary of the presentation as she walks through the sanctuary, and motions her to sit down by nodding his head at her. It is her moment to shine as she continues to walk to her assigned seat.

The First Lady has three female volunteer aides. Two aides assist when the church is not in session. These women have volunteered their precious time away from their families. Some of them babysit her children without compensation. They may have husbands, children, and jobs of their own. They may be asked at any time, day or night, to come to her aid, without compensation. They feel it is their Godly duty to serve without questioning or asking for anything in return.

The scripture Therefore, I urge you, brothers and sisters, in view of God's mercies, to offer your bodies as a living sacrifice, holy and pleasing to God this is your true and proper worship." (Romans 12:1) is used on people in the church to get them to work without compensation. People are manipulated feel guilty if they complain.

Disrespect in this church was at a high level. The Leader was a dictator; he did not accept a suggestion from any of his people.

The Fragrance

Naomi was groomed as a young child to become a Pastor's Wife. She received the Lord Jesus and joined the church choir at age eleven. Her mother gave her advice weekly. She was told by her mother to save herself for marriage. "No man would want to marry used goods," she always said. "The Lord will say something to me if someone tries to mess with you." Naomi believed her mother and made sure that a man did not go near her.

Her mother made sure that she went to charm school. She had her watch other First Ladies who were poised and proper. She learned to walk and speak as a good First Lady should. Always smile, no matter what is going on. If your husband talks evil to you in front of others, do not say anything; allow it. Never talk back to your husband. Buy the best of everything, if he can afford it.

Dress like you are a Queen; you are the best-dressed woman in the church. The other women in the church are watching you. You set the example and the tone for the church. Be watchful; never get to close to anyone in the church, especially the Sisters. Some of them will try to get information on how you care for the pastor. They do that to take your place. If you argue, do not tell anyone in the church. Find someone else to talk to. Pray for your husband without ceasing. Always feed him in the kitchen and the bedroom. If you do not, someone else will.

Remember he is in charge over you. Speak with a soft voice if you are a preacher; tone down your gift of preaching. Never out preach your husband.

One Saturday afternoon. Naomi and her mother went out to lunch. She thought it was strange that her mother pushed her to wear a dress that she wears typically to church. She also had her press her hair. "Put some grease on those lips, young lady."

"What's going on, Mother?"

"You need to look good today."

Once they arrived at the restaurant, her mother made sure there was an empty seat next to Naomi. Her other ordered three glasses of water. Naomi was distracted by a handsome man that walked through the doors of the restaurant. He was six feet four inches; a light-skinned, muscle-built hunk of a man. Naomi usually did not pay much attention to men passing by, yet when he strolled into the restaurant, his presence commanded the room. She caught a whiff of his cologne and almost moaned out loud. Did others notice him? She turned away quickly, not wanting to alarm her mother and be accused of lusting in her spirit.

To her surprise, her mother nodded to the man to sit down. Naomi almost fainted.

"Hi, my name is Calvin Michaels. Your mother has told me a lot about you."

"Hi, I am Naomi Love. She has told me nothing about you. Nice to meet you," she said as she looked at her mother, puzzled.

Calvin Michaels was as charming as he was handsome. He got her attention right away. They hit it off good. Just like Mother thought they would. He had enough charisma to charm anyone with words.

They started dating immediately. Calvin treated her like Mother said she should be treated, with dignity and respect. He was a gentleman who opened her car door for her every time she got into his car. He took her out every weekend. They started talking about marriage after six months of dating. She told him early in the dating process that she was a virgin and was saving herself for marriage. He explained to her his plans to pastor a church.

The Fragrance

Naomi and Calvin married when she was eighteen years old; he was twenty-two. They did not have a big wedding. A friend of theirs performed the ceremony at her mother's house. They began to work on the church right away. Mother was pleased. Naomi was happy, her childhood dream now a reality. Mother groomed her too well. Naomi knew it was destiny.

The church doors opened. She was excited to be the First Lady of a black Church. She did not know what to expect as the First Lady. Naomi had shopped for her new role. She'd purchased a few designer outfits from a high-end thrift shop. She wanted to be careful about spending money, yet she wanted to look good.

They named the church My Way Church of Holiness. First Lady Naomi was now a Pastor's Wife.

Fifty people joined. One of Naomi's childhood friends who joined the church called her 'Naomi.' Pastor Michaels immediately made the announcement. Do not call my bride Naomi; she is a Pastor's Wife. Call her First Lady Michaels from this day forward. It does not matter if you knew her before she was married or not. Naomi was flattered and she smiled with pride.

Pastor Michaels immediately assigned six men to be by his side like he needed protection. Armour Bearers to do as he commands them. People labeled him a preaching machine. He will preach you under a table. The Pastor and First Lady children were talented musicians and psalmists. The two young boys played instruments while the girl was a singer.

The Pastor and the First Lady agreed that she would work a full-time job. He quit his job building houses to pastor full time. The church paid him a salary. His responsibility was to take care of the church. Word got around the community that there was a new preacher in town. He was like no other, and he was going places. The fifty people who joined quickly invited everyone they knew to church. The church rapidly grew to a thousand members in one year.

The Sisters in the church became dedicated to Pastor Michaels, and wanted to please him. He was the closest thing to God for them. He made them feel good about themselves with his ability to manipulate them with his smooth words. He often complimented the sisters on their appearance and their ability to get things done. Some of the women never had anyone to treat them well, and he knew that from his private counseling sessions with them. He looked at their church membership applications to see what professional and creative abilities they had. He then assigned them according to their strengths. He also used their weakness against them when he needed them to do more than their church duties. The Pastor had the women cleaning his house running personal errands for him. Working in the name of being committed to him and the church.

The Pastor used what he knew about the lonely, confused, and mishandled women, to get them to be closer to him. His relationships were inappropriate going out with them outside of the church services, to dinners and events. He encouraged the women to work hard in the church, pressured them to invite others to join. His plan worked, the church continued to grow.

Pastor Michaels' gifts were preaching and leading people. His wife was good at music and office work. She made sure all the books were in order. First Lady kept his preaching schedule. She taught Sunday school. New female member a book keeper professionally, took over the position of keeping the books relieving the first lady. The pastor was good at placing the right people in the correct spot, the women in domestic and office jobs, the men in security positions.

The pastor was overheard flattering the single and married Sisters, telling them how good they looked in the outfits they wore. The women in the church loved the compliments of the pastor.

First Lady Michaels was a great psalmist. When she sang, the people shouted and danced. Pastor Michaels did not allow her to sing most Sundays; she got too much attention from the people. Naomi was a sweet happy lady. You never saw her without her smile. She worked hard in the church. She worked a full-time job, took care of their three children. She traveled with her husband. He had a demanding ministry schedule, services on Sunday morning 9am and evening 3pm, including Tuesday prayer night, Thursday night teaching. She did what she thought was expected of her as the wife and first lady.

She did not like her husband's flirting, she did not say anything. His flirtatious ways were evident to all. He seemed not to care what anyone thought. He was good at explaining his behavior away. "I am encouraging the women who have low self-esteem," he told her.

The church was thriving; everything was in place. The women in church whispered about the changes they began to see in First Lady Naomi. Her smile was not as bright; she did not talk as much. She wore more makeup on her face. She came to church wearing long sleeves in the summertime.

One Sunday, all were shocked to see that Lady Michaels was wearing a cast on her arm. She said that she fell down her stairs at home. Another time, she had a broken leg.

(She fell again.) Pastor Calvin yelled at her from the pulpit, saying that she can get rebuked like any other member of the church. She sat in her front seat and smiled.

Pastor's sermons were often about controlling your house. "Man should know how to control his house and wife." "Divorce is not honored by God." The rumors of him dating women in the church and community circulated in the neighborhood. The pastor was accused of several inappropriate relationships in the church by several of his female parishioners. Some of them bragged about their conquest of the pastor and the honor of being chosen. One Sunday, a female member stood up to announce that she was in love with the pastor and planned to be the First Lady of My Way Church of Holiness someday.

Sister Sylvia was a beautiful young woman in her twenties. She wore her clothes tight to reveal her firm bosom and tight young body. She recently moved from another church to join My Way Church of Holiness. Sylvia had two young boys, ages three and four. The rumor was that her husband left her because she was dating another pastor.

She met Pastor Michaels one evening at a church service where she was a member. She was intrigued by his display of power and preaching ability. Even though he was ten years her senior and married, she was hit by the lust bug and did not care about him being married.

Pastor Michaels took one look at her and the feeling was mutual. He could not speak when he was around her. Once he gained his composure, he approached her with an invitation to preach at his church. She was not a preacher, but he made her one that day.

The lust bug had him by the tail. He lusted at her beauty and youthful playfulness. Every time he said something funny, she laughed loud so he could hear her. The way she flaunted her body at the pastor as she walked across the church staring at him drove him wild with desire for her. He did not care who was watching him. At the church service that day, he preached like a wild man. As he was preaching, he was thinking about Sister Sylvia, he preached like a wild man. The people did not know what was on his mind. They commented that he never preached like that before, he preached them into a frenzy.

He told his friends that he never met a woman like her before. She did not conform to the traditions of the Church; she did her own thing. She was confident about who she was with her sexuality. He told them it would be great if she accepts being my mistress.

The Church had traditions on how the women were to dress in the church. Cultures were not for her; she paid no attention to what they wanted. Knowing how to manipulate men, she was in a relationship with her present married pastor. She could get them to do whatever she wanted, including leaving their current wife, if that was her desire.

She left her church to join My Way Church of Holiness with Pastor Michaels. She became his mistress. He set her up in an apartment, took care of the monthly rent. He purchased a new car, included monthly stipend. She wanted more. She desired to be the First Lady of the Church.

She often manipulated Pastor Michaels, testing his loyalty to her by telling lies on the members and asking him to put them out of the church. Sister Silva told the pastor once that some of the members were conspiring to take the church from him. Pastor Michaels put them out of the church escorted by his armed security staff. He told the church that whatever Sylvia said he believed – ignoring the fact that he was married. He got bold with his relationship with Sister Sylvia. People often saw him coming out of her apartment all times of the night. She had a big picture of him and her in her apartment for all to see. He became more disrespectful to his wife. Usually when he preached, First Lady Naomi was the one to introduce him to the people and give words. He began to call Sister Sylvia instead.

Things were becoming complicated for Lady Michaels at home. The pastor was spending more time with Sister Sylvia and less time with his family. People noticed them coming from airports and hotels after they took trips together. When Lady Naomi got enough courage to confront her Husband , he hit her and said that she was crazy. Lady Naomi talked with her mother about her concerns. Her mother said, "Pray about it." Naomi prayed day and night for God to intervene on her behalf and help her in her marriage. First Lady stayed up late at night to greet him; cooked and cleaned and dressed in beautiful lingerie, always smelling good with the best perfume. No matter what Lady Naomi did to get his attention, Pastor Michaels no longer had a desire to be with his wife.

They had fights weekly. Naomi was afraid of speaking for making the pastor angry. The pastor hit Naomi in her face, breaking a bone. He told the church she ran into a wall. Her mother agreed to pray with her for help. Naomi was being abused physically and mentally, regularly for a year.

Naomi decided that she had to stop the abuse. She tried to talk with Pastor Michaels about his behavior. Pastor Michaels confessed that he was in Love with Sister Sylvia and that they were in a relationship. He wanted a divorce. Pastor asked Naomi to grant a divorce. He also asked her to tell the church that the divorce was her idea. If she did not agree, Pastor Michaels would leave her nothing. Naomi decided to do as he asked.

One Sunday morning, First Lady Naomi Michaels stood up in front of the whole congregation to confess. She did not know what she was going to do with her life. She confessed that she had sinned and was no longer worthy of being the first Lady of My Way Church of Holiness. "Please forgive me. I have sinned against you and God. I will no longer be a member of My Way Church of Holiness." I am releasing my husband. She walked out of the church heartbroken, leaving the life and ministry she worked hard for.

The people were in shock. Pastor Michaels stood up and agreed with everything his wife said. The people cheered him on and said good riddance to First Lady Michaels. They stood by their pastor. No one asked any questions; it was church as usual.

Their divorce was final within a few months. Shortly after, Pastor Michaels stood up to announce that he was getting married: he and Sister Sylvia were to wed. The church members attended the wedding, as well as their children. Sister Sylvia was now First Lady Sylvia Michaels. She immediately had him buy her the house of her dreams. Sylvia moved out of her old home, purchased new furniture. The church budget paid for everything. She quit her job, getting ready to be a sit-down First Lady of My Way Holiness Church.

Things were going well for the newlyweds. They traveled often and enjoyed life. One stormy Sunday after church, Pastor Calvin Michaels and First Lady Sylvia Michaels were on their way to one of their favorite dinner restaurants. They were smiling and enjoying each other's company. Pastor Michaels was driving, and she was under his arm. It was raining hard. A bad storm unexpectedly hit the area, and he was unable to see in front of him due to the hard rain coming down.

Pastor Michaels stopped at a red light. He thought the light turned green, but it was still red. He moved out into oncoming traffic and was fatally hit by a large truck. He and First Lady Silva Michaels were dead on impact.

STORY NUMBER TWO
Unfilled

Lolita, a licensed Minister, was well off financially, lived in a beautiful home in California, and drove a high-end Mercedes. She traveled, preaching the gospel of Jesus to different parts of the country. She was a full-time Minister, and made her money speaking. Minister Lolita was happy with her life except for one area: relationships with men. She wanted a happy marriage that would complete her. "Coming full circle," is what Lolita called it. She did not have much luck in relationships.

She was married four times, all failures, as she talks in her head about the relationships.

There were problems with the men she married. The memories of the alcoholic drug-dealing addict sadden me. Number two abused her, cheating with other women and men. The last one had a disease called lazy.

Whenever the relationship did not go as she wanted it to go, she got divorced and tried again.

Her mother said to her once, "Be like Elizabeth Taylor. Keep trying, maybe one day you will get it right." Minister Lolita looked like the perfect catch. She was five feet, four inches, bright skin like the men liked. Shaped like a Coca-Cola bottle and could preach the pants off any man. She was self-sufficient. She had a great personality – outgoing and friendly, yet a humble spirit. She had a challenge staying with the men she dated when she found a flaw in the men. After dating six months she determined whether they were up to her standards.

She refused to give up on love. When she was home for her rest periods from preaching, she was at her church, ironically named the Church of Love. She never told anyone she had married four times. She knew if they found out about her past relationships, criticism would come with their self-righteous, religious babble. She kept her life private from the church members. She did not make friends, wanting to be left alone to worship and go home.

Lolita's pastor was a handsome, charming man. He was a homebody; his concerns were God, family, and church. If he was not in church, he was helping in the community. He was a quiet, humble soul a well-known pastor with a good reputation. A widower for a year, all the single women in the church wanted to marry him. They showed him a lot of attention to prove they were to be the next first lady of the church. He wanted to remarry. He did not pursue any of the women; he kept himself busy until he found the right wife. He was not interested in the woman who tried to pursue him. That was against his belief. He lived by the scripture, "He who finds a wife finds a good thing and receives favor from the Lord." (Proverbs 18:22 NIV)

He pastored a church of five thousand members. When Lolita joined the church, she explained to him her reason for being there. She was not able to attend every Sunday; she had a ministry of her own that kept her on the road.

Lolita explained to the pastor that she planned to attend Sunday services during her rest from travelling. He agreed to her terms. The For three years she was a member. She sent in her tithes and giving offerings to the church, feeling it was her duty to support the church that feeds her the word of God. When she was there, she sat in the second row. She loved his preaching. He was a good teacher; no showing off, just taught the word of God. She got what she needed when she was home. She did not make many friends. She said that she did not have time for nonsense, just wanted God. Wanted to get her soul refreshed to go back into the world and preach.

Travelling the airways and highways, Lolita met a lot of men. She went on dates when she wanted to. Minister Lolita met interesting men from all over the world. She had many proposals for her hand in marriage.

Several men from Africa wanted to marry her. She figured they needed a green card. Lolita was introduced to men from China, Italy, Europe, and Canada. She had great experiences meeting the different cultures of men. Minister Lolita loved dating. Lolita had to admit to herself that she was attracted mostly to men in the United States. She loved the men in California the most, where there were many facets to the men. She enjoyed the intelligent conversation.

She had a problem with her emotions. If she felt them getting too close to her, she shied away with fear. She had made many mistakes in her previous marriages and did not want to go down that road again. Upon getting to know them, she always found something wrong. Lolita did not like when the man talked too much about himself, was uneducated, or had low standards.

She did not date men with children. She believed in love and marriage and wanted to be careful not to mess up again.

She prayed and asked God to send her the man of her dreams. She had a list that she kept in her purse of what her ideal man might be. Whenever she went out, she discreetly compared her list to the man she went out with.

Lolita's List for Perfect Man

> Job making six figures
> Be kind
> Good sense of humor
> Not dull
> Love the Lord
> Living for God for real not faking to be a Christian
> Not take himself too seriously
> Relatively handsome, not shabby
> Must have his own money
> Intelligence a must, not arrogant

I want my mate to understand that I have a ministry of my own. I do not want to marry, a pastor. A pastor's wife has too much pressure trying to please everyone and sacrificing her desires and dreams. I do not plan to share my husband with the world. As a minister who travels, when I go home, I want to rest, do not want my phone ringing because members are having problems and want him to leave his family to be with them.

Lolita decided to go online and date. She began to correspond with a gentleman from New York. Minister Willie Williams. He had his own house, Associate Minister at his church. She had a conviction about not wanting to date pastors but took a chance. She was lonely. He looked good online. He was handsome: lighted skinned with green eyes, six feet two inches and slim built, intelligent with a master's degree. After a few months of talking, Lolita's birthday came up on June 26; she was turning forty-five years old. To her surprise, Minister Willie Williams sent her a bouquet of red roses and candy, along with three-hundred-dollar check attached.

She was happy as well as surprised. While they were on their live phone time, Willie told her to put on a pretty dress that was tight and take a picture with her roses and candy, and holding up the check. She did not own anything short. Lolita compromised with a dress that was in her closet, with a shorter than comfortable length. Lolita felt uneasy about the request, yet she complied. The dress fit her shapely body. She texted the pictures to him; he loved the pictures.

"When will you be able to visit me, Willie?"

"In two months, I will be free."

"Free from what?"

"Oh, just free to travel."

"Oh, ok." She dismissed what he said even though it sounded strange to her. They continued their relationship by phone. Willie decided that it was time for them to meet in person. Lolita was excited because they had been talking on the phone for six months.

He would be here within the week. She was happy.

She told Pastor McLand that a friend of hers was about to visit from New York. She made him aware of her plans in case something terrible might happen to her. Willie announced his travel plans to drive from New York. Why in the world was he driving that far? What about a plane? Willie drove for a week from New York to California.

She gave him her address. He told her he did not want to go to her house right away, so they met at a hotel. She went to his room, which was furnished with two queen size beds. They greeted each other with a kiss. Something was off in his embrace; she dismissed it. She did not feel the chemistry from the kiss like she thought she would. He was planning to stay at the hotel for the duration of his trip. She decided to stay over with him for the night. They slept in separate beds. He did not make an advance toward her; she thought that strange since technically they had been dating for six months. She dismissed that thought.

Lolita went home the following day from her visit with Willie. She was happy to take off for a month from her preaching assignments. She invited her guest Minister Willie to intend church with her. She introduced him to her church family as a family friend from New York.

Pastor Robert McLand did not like him and said so. "There is something strange about him." "What is it?" Lolita asked.

"I am not able to put my finger on it, and the Lord has not revealed anything to me."

Lolita dismissed his comment and went home.

That Monday, while she was home, someone showed up in her yard with a moving U-Haul. What in the world was going on? When the man stepped out of the truck, she saw that it was Willie. What was he doing?

"Hi girl, I wanted this to be a surprise. I decided to move to California to be closer to you." He was excited as he began to unload the moving van.

"Ok, that is good. Why do you have a moving van?"

"I have not secured my apartment yet and thought you would be kind enough to allow me to stay with you for a month."

Lolita stood in her driveway, shocked, no words coming out of her mouth. She gained her composure to speak. "You can stay for a month. You cannot bring your belongings, just the clothes needed for the month." Whew, she said it and waited for his response. *What in the world will the people at church think of me? I am not going to tell anyone that this man is staying with me.* He became silent for a few minutes and said, "Ok, I will be back." He drove away.

Two hours later Willie returned without the U-Haul. He was driving a black Cadillac, clean as the board of health. *Where did he get it?* Lolita greeted Willie, "Nice car."

"Yes, I had it in storage."

Storage, hmm, she thought. She invited him into her ranch house. She had three bedrooms and three full baths. He was impressed by her home. "This is, ah, nice, Lolita." She escorted him to the guest room. "You may stay here for a month."

He was with her for a week without incident. When Willie went out, Lolita went into the guest room and went through his belongings. In his overnight bag was a pamphlet about AIDS and the cure. What frightened were the discharge papers from jail. She became nervous. *What have I got involved in?* When he returned, she did not discuss it with him.

Lolita invited Minister Willie to church on Sunday, but he declined her offer. "I do not like your pastor; something is wrong with him." She said, "Ok," and went to church. Upon her return from church, she smelled food cooking. He cooked dinner. He went into her large freezer, cooked two steaks and three lobsters. The kitchen was a mess with dishes, flour, and pots all over the place. She pretended it was ok. She wondered why he used her food, why not buy his own food, and cook it? Three weeks went by with no offer from him to pay for his stay or the use of her house. He watched porn all day. He kept her house dirty. It was unnerving.

This way of living was all wrong for Lolita. Lolita went to her guest room to speak with Minister Williams about how he was using her food and not keeping her house clean. He was on his laptop.

"What are you watching Lolita asked? She noticed it was porn. she was irritated

"Yes, come in porn is ok, Watch with me." She sat on the bed for a few minutes, then left the room sickened by what she saw.

He followed behind her; she sat in the kitchen. "I was thinking. I am called to be a Pastor and looking for a First Lady to help me start my church. I know that you have yourself together, and it will not be hard for us to come up with the money. You would make a great First Lady." Lolita nodded in response. She was married four times in the past. She was not about to make another big mistake.

"We will see." She went to her room, locked the door and went to sleep. The next day was Willie's birthday. Wanting to be kind, she presented him with a card with fifty dollars in it. He opened the card and yelled, "Fifty dollars! I gave you three hundred for your birthday, you ungrateful woman. Your gift is stupid." Lolita was shocked. He continued to carry on with angry words. "Here I am staying with you, trying to treat you right, and you give me fifty dollars for my birthday. You are full of crap. You do not know a man when you see one. Stupid."

How in the world am I going to get this man out of my house? She could not tell anyone to help her because he was a secret. She was embarrassed and a bit nervous. *Lord, help me.*

"Did the Lord tell you, Minister Willie, to curse me with that mouth of yours, 'preacher'?" "Forget you, stupid woman. I am out of here." And just like that, he was gone.

Thank God. She cleaned her house, then decided she needed a relaxing atmosphere. *I need a tasty filet mignon.* She got dressed up and took the hour-long ride to her favorite steak restaurant. As she was standing in the line, she heard a voice say, "What you are doing here alone?" It was Pastor McLand.

"Hi, Pastor. I needed to get out. I love this place."

"It's my favorite steak restaurant as well, Sister Lolita."

She looked around to see who was with him. "Are you alone?"

"Yes, Why? I am not dating anyone. You?"

She cleared her throat, "No."

"She will be seated with me," he instructed the maître d'. She smiled, following his lead. "Are you ok, Sister Lolita?"

"Yes, of course, Pastor."

"Call me Robert."

"Ok, call me Lolita." As they waited for their drinks, Lolita asked, "Pastor, tell me something. Why haven't you remarried?"

"I have not found the right woman."

"You do know the ladies in the church are waiting for you to pick one of them," she smiled.

"I know. What about you, Lolita?" She held her head down in shame. She never told anyone about her previous marriages that only lasted six months each.

"Pastor," Lolita paused and took a deep breath. "I am ashamed of my past; I have been married four times. I have made a mess of my relationships with men. I cannot blame everything on them. I made the wrong decisions. Three of my marriages lasted six months, one three months."

Pastor McLand looked in her eyes as if he were trying to reach her soul. He touched her hand ever so softly, "Lolita," he said with a soft voice that touched her soul and emotions. "You have nothing to be ashamed of. They were not right for you. God gives us many changes in life repeatedly."

She looked at him with tearstained eyes. "Thank you, Robert." They talked for hours enjoying each other's company and a great meal. He paid for the food and escorted her to the car.

He asked her out many more times as they got closer.

Lolita invited him to her house for a home-cooked meal. She played soft music. Before she realized what was happening, they were in her bed; she had the best night of passion she ever had in her life.

She told him that she had to be away for six months out of the country. As she sat on the plane, she knew she had fallen for the pastor. She always said that she did not want to be with a Pastor. She believed God had plans for her life beyond her control. She shook her head to dismiss him from her mind. She did not want to get deep into a relationship with the pastor. She already had to pray and ask God to forgive her for sleeping with him.

Lolita needed to concentrate on her work ahead of her ministry. There was no word from the pastor. The trip was successful. People got the help they needed through her preaching. *I will not call him,* she thought. *I am upset but must move on. I do not think I will go back to the church; it is too awkward. I cannot face Pastor Michael.* Her phone rang; it was nosey Sis Jenkins.

"Girl, you are not going to believe this. How are you doing?"

"Hi, Sister Jenkins, what is it?"

"You are not going to believe this. The Pastor announced that he is getting married."

"What did you say?"

"You heard me, girl. Married. Announced that he met a wonderful woman, it was time for him to be happy again. He knows for sure she is the one God sent to him.."

"Thank you, Sister Jenkins. Bye."

Lolita's heart sank with disappointment. Against her better judgement, she had fallen in love with Pastor Michael McLand. That was her punishment for sleeping with him. She cried on the drive home from the airport.

Upon arriving home, she did not bother to unpack her suitcase, and went to bed early. She got up at sunrise, not well rested, and decided to pray to ask God for directions. She felt as if she failed God and herself. She prayed for God's peace.

She got dressed and decided to go shopping. She opened her door, and there was a large white box with a big red bow on her steps. She checked for a note, but there was none. "*I pray that crazy Willie did not leave the package. If he comes back here, I am going to call the police. No label. I do not remember ordering anything,*" she thought.

She set the box in the house, she planned to shopping. When she opened the door again to leave, Pastor McLand was standing in the doorway. Confused, she asked, "What are you doing here?"

"I am here to see you, Lolita. Did you get my box?"

"Your box?"

"Yes, Lolita."

Lolita was confused and unable to talk reply.

"Open the box, Lolita."

"Why?"

"There is something in there for you."

She opened the box and inside of the large box was a small black velvet box. She gasped for breath and almost passed out. "What is this?"

He took the box from her, opening it. Inside was the most beautiful five-carat princess cut ring she had ever laid her eyes on.

All of a sudden, he got down on one knee.

"What are you doing?"

"Will you marry me, Lolita? I knew after our first night out together that you were the woman for me. Will you be my wife?"

She screamed, "Yes!" They embraced and kissed. She finally found her man in Pastor McLand.

STORY NUMBER THREE
Betrayal

Ann Dickson: a healthy, plump, country girl. That's how people described her. Weighing one hundred and eighty pounds, five feet six inches, born and raised in South Carolina; attending church was her life.

After graduating from high school, she went on to get her certificate as a nursing assistant. Her desire was to get married to a good man and settle down with three or more children. She dated and married her high school sweetheart Charles Swenson, who was also a member of her church. They were in love and looked like a good fit for each other. They started their family right away; she gave birth to four children. Her husband, Charles, worked as a school custodian. He was active in church, taught Sunday school, and was a deacon, the next phase as far she was concerned would be pastor. She sang in the choir faithfully. Secretly she prayed for her husband to become a pastor.

Charles told Ann the Lord said he is to pastor a church. They did not have much money, but they were in love and felt they could do anything. They prayed together and said that the Lord would provide a way for them. Ann was happy; her prayers answered. They spoke with their leader at church and got his blessings. The church where they were members gave them a thousand dollars to start the church. They searched and found a mobile home in South Carolina.

They prepared the building to look like a church. They worked hard together for months getting the church ready for the opening date. They were excited about doing the work of the Lord.

The doors of the church opened in late June; the sign placed on the door read: All Are Welcome to Love Will Prevail Church of God. The small building was able to hold fifty people comfortably. When the doors opened, twenty people joined. They were happy. After a month, ten young women in their early twenties.

Ann Dickson Swenson was now somebody special. She was the First Lady of a black Church. Ann worked hard to make the church look beautiful. She wanted to be the best at her role in being an excellent example for the church and her pastor husband. She was happy, and the church was an atmosphere of love. Everyone got along well. The people loved Pastor Swenson's personality. The way he taught the gospel, letting them know that everyone is to be loved and to share what you have with someone in need. The people began to count on the pastor for everything; they never made a move without telling him first. He began to like the way they treated and relied on him. He did not ask for the control; he did not deny the position.

After a year as pastor, her husband changed. He became high-minded, stubborn, and arrogant.

Her husband insisted that she start calling him Pastor Swenson, even at home. She did not think anything of it;

most of the First Ladies she knew called their husbands 'Pastor' at church.

The young ladies called her house late at night without acknowledging her and ask for the pastor. She always handed him the phone as he walked into another room to talk to them. "Do you mind Charles," (He interrupted, "Pastor Swenson.") "Do you mind Pastor Swenson, asking the people not to call so late? It interrupts our family time."

"Yes I do, Sister Ann. When they need me, I will answer." Ann walked away so as not to start an argument in front of the children.

The calls at night became more frequent. The pastor's attitude got worse, disrespectful. He quit his job without telling Ann; decided he needed to be at church full time. "Charles, we have only been pastoring for a year," Ann proclaimed.

"Well, I am pastoring, not you."

"Why are you quitting your job? The church is not bringing in much money right now to support us."

"If you quit your job, it will be a financial strain on your family and Church."

"The church is not bringing in enough money to give you a salary, Charles," Ann argued again. Pastor Charles Dickson Swenson said, "You are working. God will provide." He took a salary from the church against his wife's advice. He bought a couple of new suits with the church money, putting a strain on his family and the church. It was a good thing most of the fifty members were helping to pay the bills of the church. The members were everyday working-class people; they did not have a lot of money. They had faith in their leader to treat them well.

Pastor Swenson began strutting around the church like he owned the world. The women in the church began to take notice of him more. Flirting and telling him how good he was looking.

He loved the attention from the women at church. He paid less attention to his wife and more attention to the women at church. There were times he would leave their bed late at night to meet with a female member who claimed to have an emergency. There was one member that called more than the others. She was demanding, never giving her name. "Let me speak to Charles now; he knows my name." Ann got tired and hung up on the woman that night. The aggravated First Lady went to bed early.

She understood that women would be after her man. One of her biggest challenges was fighting off the evil that took over some of the women – She wondered why some women thought marrying a Pastor was a prize to be won.

Ann got up on Sunday, not feeling much like going to church. Not going was not an option she had. When Ann got to the church's door, she stopped for a minute. *Help me, Lord.* Ready, set, action, she pushed the door open and went in.

The usher called for testimony time. "Does anyone want to stand and tell how good God has been to you?" It was a time when the members stood up to announce what the Lord had done for them, and how they made it through hard times.

A pretty twenty-something young girl stood up wearing a short dress. She was pregnant. "Giving honor to God, who is the head of my life. Giving honor to my Pastor Charles Swenson, my baby daddy." She looked at Pastor and screamed for all to hear. "Charles, when are you going to leave her?" Everyone turned to look at her with shock, then turned their attention to the pastor. One of the Mothers of the Church went to reach for the young woman to shut her up. The pastor said, tone sharp, "Mother, sit down. Leave her alone." The pregnant woman blurted out, "Charles, you said you were leaving her soon." First Lady Swenson looked at her husband, Pastor Swenson. The pastor stood there for a few minutes, looking confused. "Charles," the young pregnant girl said, "It is her or me."

"Charles," his wife said again, looking puzzled and worried. Their four young children, aged two to ten, were at church listening and watching what was going on.

The pastor, after what seemed to be an hour, finally spoke up as everyone watched and waited for his response. "Sorry, Ann," he said in a low voice, "I choose Gloria."

"What!" First Lady screamed, about to faint. The usher had to hold her up. One of the Sisters in the Church took her children to the back of the church, to protect them. "What you mean you choose Gloria? Is this bad joke? Who is she? Why, When Charles?"

"No," Gloria added "This is not a joke. This is my church now" Pastor said be quiet Gloria I will handle Ann."

"Handle Ann,'" said First Lady Swenson, "What do you mean, 'handle Ann'? I am your wife, twelve years! We have four children together, and a home." She got out of her seat with tear-stained eyes and reached toward Gloria, the pregnant lady. "I will tear you apart and rip that bastard out of your stomach."

"Stop the First Lady," the pastor said, "Put her out of the church." The two deacons reluctantly went toward the First Lady and put her out, kicking and screaming. The children ran after her crying.

"Good!" exclaimed Gloria, the pastor's pregnant mistress. "I am the First Lady now," and she sat down as if she was taking her throne. Half the people walked out that day.

Pastor Swenson went home and packed his bags; he refused to discuss anything with his wife. "I am leaving you for Gloria, Sorry. I love her. She understands me, and she will push me to greatness. Gloria listens to me, keeps herself looking good."

The humiliation and betrayal put Ann in a deep state of depression. She was unable to care for her children. She failed to pay for her household bills, and moved in with her mother. The heartache was more than she could handle. She was unable to sleep or eat. She thought about it for weeks. *What did I do wrong? How did I miss the signs of his cheating and being unhappy with me? His position of being a pastor went to his head. Maybe I should not have prayed for my husband to be a pastor.*

Weeks turned into months, no word from Charles. He had not so much as called to check on his children. Anne thought she was going to lose her mind; she loved her husband despite his betrayal of her and their children. She prayed for the Lord to help her. *Please, Lord, take this pain away. Show me how to heal. Help me take care of my children. I want my family back. Bring my husband back home. Lord. I forgive my husband for hurting the children and me.* Months turned into a year. A first lady who heard about what happened to her visited her and prayed with Ann.

She convinced First Lady Ann Swenson to go with her, to have the saints pray for her. Ann had not been in church for a year. She was embarrassed about her situation, and did not want people gossiping about her. When she arrived at the church with her First Lady friend, the saints gathered around her with love. They prayed that her emotions would get better. She decided to stay at that church and heal.

In the meantime, Pastor Charles Swenson was having trouble of his own in his new life. Most of the members left the Church. He had five people left. He was not able to pay the bills at the church. The money from the church dried up. He was not able to keep his mistress the way she wanted.

Gloria argued with Charles day and night about money. "Push the people who are left to give more. What happened to you? You were a better man when I first met you. You promised me that I was going to be the First Lady. You promised me cars and money. Look at you, you cannot take care of yourself. Let me tell you, Charles. I am not pregnant, Get out of my house and don't come back."

"But Gloria, where will I go? Besides, I am paying for this house."

"I do not care where you go. Return to her with your sorry self."

The pastor was in a sad state. He went to the church where his wife was. He asked the pastor if he could have words. He stood in front of the congregation and begged for forgiveness. "I repent of my sins; I cheated on my wife. Please take me back, Ann." Everyone looked to see what she would do. Pastor nudged Ann to walk toward him, to go to him. She walked toward him and they embraced. She allowed him back in her life. He returned home to his family. Pastor Swenson went back to work full time. Both of them returned to the church they started together. The five faithful members keep things going until the return of their pastor. Things were going slow, yet functioning.

After two months, Gloria showed up outside the church doors. She apologized for putting him out. She wanted Charles back; she confessed her love for him. He did not know what to do. Gloria had his mind confused.

When First Lady Ann went outside to see what was taking him so long, he was gone.

First Lady Ann turned around and went back into the church. She and the children went home. After a couple of days, she realized that he was not coming back. He called and said, "I am sorry Ann. I cannot help myself. I am back with Gloria."

This time, Ann decided she was not losing her mind. The pain hit her heart like a knife; she did not give up. Strength came when she prayed.

The pastor left the church and his family again. Lady Ann remembered she worked hard to open the church and was not going to abandon the people that the Lord sent there. She started preaching on Sundays, and the Church grew. She changed the paperwork on the church to have her name on all documents. She filed for a divorce. Ann was able to buy the building they were renting. She sold the property to another pastor named Paul Roy. Ann decided to build a church from the ground. She kept the name Love will prevail Church of God. God was good to her allowed her to keep her mind. The love of Jesus never left her. She started working full time as the pastor, and the membership grew to two hundred people. She was a good pastor.

Minister Paul Roy the builder of her church visits and joins her church. Ann notices his kindness he is gentle with her children and the people in the church. He was helpful to Pastor Ann. Minister Paul Roy helped her in the ministry. Minister Roy was forty years old, never married before. He was a soft-spoken man with wisdom and strength. They got close to each other, Roy loved her and the children; they decided to marry. The ceremony was beautiful, with all the members in attendance.

BETRAYAL

Pastor Ann's new husband Pastor Paul Roy was up teaching in the church, the atmosphere was high. People in the church were happy and praising God.

Her ex husband Charles decided to visit the church against the advice of one of his friends. He walked down the aisle to the altar after the church was over without an invite. Charles went up thinking that Pastor Paul Roy was the Lead Minister of the church.

Pastor Paul Roy allowed him to approach the altar. He said he had a confession to make. "I ignored the warnings from my wife. I left home, destroyed my family for another woman. I demolished everything the Lord gave me. I became deceived by a woman who was a witch. When I came to senses, I lost everything. I am glad that the Lord did not kill me. I am here because I cannot rest. I must make things right with my wife, my children and the Lord.

The biggest mistake of his life, I made more than once."

Pastor Ann Roy sat in her seat listening, no expression on her face. It surprised everyone when Charles pointed to Ann. "She was my wife," Then to his four children. He cried and begged for forgiveness from Pastor Ann Roy.

Pastor Paul Roy asked for Pastor Ann to come forth. Pastor Roy said, "Is this the family?" Charles Swenson responded, "Yes."

"She told me her story of how you left her and the children. She forgives you." Ann shook her head in agreement with her husband. "Sir, you are too late. She is my wife now, and I am not leaving her or our children. Please leave the church. You are not welcome here anymore. We will continue to pray for you."

People in the congregation clapped as Charles was escorted out of the church doors, never to be seen again.

STORY NUMBER FOUR
The Perfect Couple

Pastor Larry and First Lady Daisy Jones were the perfect couple. World-travelled and well known for their unique style of ministry. The teaching techniques taught couples how to have a relationship based on love connections. They serviced organizations that wanted to show excellence in relationships. They were popular. Organizations needed to book and plan a year to get them. They spoke at churches and organizations all over the world. They were paid ten thousand dollars, minimum, for speaking engagements. They often spoke of their Godly assignment, including coaching couples how to their love partner.

The Jones pastored a mega five thousand members plus church in Virginia for fifteen years. They can be seen on significant gospel television and radio shows throughout the country. Their books and products produce millions of dollars. They ran charities for their community to help feed the hungry. If you wanted advice on how to keep your marriage happy and stable, they were the gurus on the subject. Many churches followed their lead on teaching relationship classes.

The Jones met in college, had been married for twenty years, and produced three children who are now adults. They have four grandchildren. They live in luxury with a four million dollar, five thousand square foot magnificent estate in Virginia, with a paneled library, five bedrooms with a powder room for each bedroom, formal garden, with a luxurious heated pool.

The Jones were the example of a successful marriage. They were as attractive as they were wealthy and talented. Women drooled when they saw him, wishing they were in his wife's place. Men tried not to look at her, but it was impossible to do. She was beautiful, magnificently dressed all the time.

They loved each other and showed it by public displays of affection, which made people more covetous of the relationship, wishing their husband or wife were like they were them. Their mission in life, which they discussed at every seminar and conference, was to display love, especially in public. "It is ok to touch your partner in public in a respectful way," as he kissed First Lady Jones. "It is ok to tell your partner how much you love and appreciate them," as she looked at him sweetly. "I love you, babe."

The Jones travelled all over the globe preaching the Gospel of Jesus speaking on love and relationships. Couples learned techniques on keeping fire and romance going even though they are believers. They wanted to prove a believer's passion and caring for their spouse was part of holy living.

The Jones demonstrated techniques such as couples holding hands while looking into each other's eyes. This caused couples to get closer. Then they would ask them to tell each other why they married them.

The Jones were holding a secret of domestic abuse within their perfect relationship. The husband beat First Lady Daisy Jones. After successful conferences, on the flight or drive back home, Daisy often encountered beatings from her perfect pastor husband. He accused her of flirting with strangers or glancing too long at a man and smiling longer than professionally necessary.

If someone mistakenly touched or brushed past Daisy, the pastor became furious. He beat her until she was unable to move for days. The black and blue bruises, the mental abuse, no one saw. She had to endure her feelings of being hurt by herself. Daisy dared not tell anyone for fear of losing everything. Pastor Mike threatened that if she told anyone, he would kill her for sure.

Daisy smiled like she was happy while crying on the inside, and preached when needed someone to preach to her. She taught others concerning what was missing in her own relationship – love. Ministering with a broken heart. Daisy was becoming mentally unstable. She did not know what to do. Crying, when they were not preaching, in her own time.

How did we get here? For the first five years of our marriage, things were great. He was kind and loving and to me. He abused me physically always sorry. "I have never hit a woman before." I forgave him. I also promised myself that it would never happen again.

After it continued to happen, he said that I caused it. He told me I triggered him to hit me. I searched myself for the triggers. What could I do to not make him mad at me? He was not able to tell me the triggers. He got angry when I asked about them. "Do not make me mad."

After beating her, her husband begged for forgiveness. He cried, gave her gifts. His sorrowful tears were asking for forgiveness. He exclaimed his love for her, telling her how she made him crazy. Daisy felt terrible that she caused him to hurt her. Larry was unable to help himself. "You make me beat you, Daisy. You drive me mad. I love you so much I want to die sometimes."

The biggest conference of their career came up. Pastor and Lady Jones were excited. The plan to take a vacation after the event. Each of the Jones had time to speak for one hour. A fee of thirty thousand dollars would be paid to each one.

Daisy was happy about the individual paycheck. She planned to take her money and leave. She was going the leave the big house, car, money, everything, and go where Larry was not able to find her. The luxurious all-inclusive spa, in Hawaii was the perfect romantic spot. The church that hired them paid all their expenses for a week's visit.

Romance was far from Daisy's mind. She planned to tell her husband in Hawaii that she wanted a divorce; she had divorce papers with her for him to sign. She no longer wanted to live a lie. No more beatings – she wanted to be free. She wanted the voice she heard in her heart to be heard. Maybe she would be able to help women going through what she put up with for nineteen years.

She loved Larry; she gave him all of herself. She had for twenty years, four children. She gave her life to the public and a man that beat her. She had no more strength to continue the charade.

The night of the conference was spectacular. After she spoke, people gave her a standing ovation. Daisy looked over at the people clapping and cheering. Larry stood, not clapping. An uneasiness hit her spirit, and when she looked into his eyes, there was rage. Daisy had seen him jealous before; this was different. She understood surely more than ever what she needed to do. While they were on the plane, she got the nerve to talk. Larry, I need to speak to you."

"What is it, Daisy? I am tired."

"Me too, Larry."

He looked at her to get a better understanding due to her tone of voice.

She swallowed hard three times. Larry, I want a divorce."

He was silent for a long time. He did not look upset or worried. He pulled her face with his hand close to his. He was squeezing her jaw as she felt her teeth ache. He smiled kissed her lips, with a whisper, "Before I let you go, I will kill you, do you hear me?"

Daisy shook her head, yes. She felt like she just lost her freedom.

She woke up the next morning feeling drained. Her head was spinning from a conversation on the plane. Daisy was confused. *What am I going to do?* She did not know what to do. She did not have any help, and she told no one what she was going through. *I must get out of here. He has hurt me for the last time.*

She packed a small bag, got her keys, and went to her Mercedes. As she punched the keyring to open the door, she felt Paul Larry grab her by her shoulder, "Where are you going, Daisy?"

"Let me go, Larry. I need to leave. I cannot live like this anymore." She pushed him away and tried to get into her vehicle. They struggled for a minute. Suddenly Larry grabbed her and forced her to the ground. She struggled to fight his grip on her. He was too strong. While she was on the ground, he placed his hands around her neck and squeezed. She felt the pressure of his hands cut off her breath. *Larry, why?* His face was enraged as he pressed his hands tighter and tighter around her neck. Never explaining his actions, chanting, "I love you, Daisy."

The grip became tighter while Daisy gasped for air. She tried to loosen his grip but could not, choking, going in and out of consciousness. Daisy tried with all her might to fight for her life. She knew this was the end as her life came flashing before her. She was thinking about her family. Raising her children and taking care of her home, husband, and working for the Lord in ministry.

She prayed to God for the forgiveness of any wrongdoings she has committed. As she fought back, she was no match for the pressure squeezing her neck and the lack of air cutting off her breathing. Terror enters her mind and then peace. After a few minutes, she felt herself blacking out. She stopped fighting and breathing.

Larry felt the life leave Daisy's limp body. He released his grip; she was dead. Pastor Larry Jones needed to do something with the lifeless body. He felt nothing as he looked down at the dead body. The pastor opened the trunk of his car and dumped her in it, then went golfing.

STORY NUMBER FIVE
My Marriage Mate

First Lady Tina pretended not to be hurt; Pastor Henry pretended not to see her pain. He loved his movies more than he valued his relationship with his wife, Tina. All she ever wanted to be loved, safe.

Tina, a fun-loving stay at home wife in her fifties. In her second marriage. The first one ended in divorce. I saved myself for ten years before I met Henry. Henry was a kind, hard-working man. Henry worked from sunup until sundown. He pastored a congregation of people that had been with him for twenty or more years.

People in our town respected my husband. No one has ever said a bad word about him. He was attentive to his congregation. He was a giving, loving man. He would give you the shirt off his back.

Tina was determined to make her marriage work. "I cannot fail this marriage. Admittedly, I will get it right this time. I will do whatever it takes to make this marriage last forever," she sobs as she lays on the couch of her psychotherapist. "We have been married for ten years now. When I first met Henry, he was not able to keep his hands off me. He paid attention to me, told he loved me every day. We often sat on the sofa together, just holding each other. I do not know what happened to us. Where did I go wrong? I feel bad about complaining," she told her therapist.

"Most of the time, I do not allow it to bother me. I go about my day without a care. I keep myself busy with the house and community work. I pretend that I do not need intimacy. I have chosen to stay because I love Henry. I have invested too much in this relationship to leave. I used to think about the lack of intimacy every day. I believe that something is wrong with me. I consider myself attractive. I keep myself up.

"I had to think hard about what was important to me. Who wants to be in a loveless relationship? I once thought it was a deal-breaker no romance. After much thought and prayer, I realize that love is not having intimacy with your partner alone. I have trained my body not to want private time with my husband. I am married to the best roommate; we sleep in the same bed when he comes to bed. For years I felt undesirable, unattractive, and unwanted." When I Talked with my therapist she helped me to realize that my husband's lack of affection was not my fault.

I spoke with Henry often about what is going on between us. He says he does not know, but he will try to do better. I offered for us to see a relationship counselor, but he does not believe we need it. He says he will change. When I touch any part of his body, I can feel him cringe. I could touch his hand, and he flinches. Makes me feel awful inside. What is wrong to the point that you cannot have a touch anywhere on your body from your wife?

I thought maybe Henry is having an affair and does not want me. In that case, I would give him his freedom without a fight. There were times when I felt like I would have been better single. I considered leaving Henry. He is no trouble, and we laugh all the time. We do not argue, we go places together, the only thing missing is the intimacy, so I chose to stay. I deal with my emotions, desiring his touch.

Henry is a good marriage mate. I call him that because he is not my roommate because I am married to him. I created the term marriage mate. When you are in a marriage without intimacy, everything else is fine. I wonder how many women are going through this same scenario, for different reasons.

If Henry got physically sick and was not able to be with me, I would not leave. He is ill; I am not going anywhere. I am not interested in dating or starting over. I will never marry again. I love sleeping beside him when he comes to bed at times. The benefits of having him outweigh the problem.

Each person in a relationship must weigh their situation. No one can tell you what will work for you. We must all decide on our life path. I drive my dream vehicle, the ultimate Range Rover; I live comfortable in a big beautiful home, with a live-in housekeeper. I do charity work to keep busy. I no longer allow my mind to dwell on what I am missing. I look at all that I have. I am blessed.

My compromise outweighs me going back to the single life. Therefore, I accept the lack of intimacy. At times I feel lonely and yearn for a touch from him. I pray, and God comforts me. We all have things that we must deal with that are not favorable. Things that bring us pain and heartache. "The righteous person, may have many troubles, But the Lord delivers him from them all." Psalm (34:19 NIV)

People look at me and are envious, especially the women in the church. They lust after my husband. Many of them are not able to endure what I go through. You must be committed to God and the people to be a pastor's wife. My husband is a good pastor, and he takes care of the people. I tolerated his imperfections. I dare not shame him him or the Church by telling people my business.

When I feel weak, I set my mind on Jesus. "Set your thoughts on things above, not on earthly things." (Colossians 3:2 NIV) I must keep my mind pure in order not to stray. The lifestyle he affords me is not enough to keep me happy; I must commit myself to the Lord to be maintained. The material things make it easier to stay. If I were not comfortable and mature in the Lord, I would leave. Everyone must decide whether or not they can live with the situations dealt with them. I have decided to be happy in this state.

I ask myself what I can do to make my marriage better. Henry does not kiss me hug or touch me. On top of that, he is jealous if he thinks my mind is on another man. If I talk about another man, he reads into it something it is not. I must be careful around other men not to socialize too much.

I wonder how he can be jealous of a woman he does not touch. There are times when I am overwhelmed, and I feel like blasting him about our situation. I do not want to hurt him, even though I am hurting.

Every human being desires to be held, caressed. We nuzzle our children in our arms because it is comforting for them and us. Touches display love. Henry is a great husband and pastor. The congregation loves him. Henry is an excellent provider. No problem with him taking care of our finances. I do did not have to work an outside job. I do not want for money.

Lady Tina was secretly visiting with her therapist for a year. She desperately sought strength to handle her emotions. First Lady Tina read her Bible daily to help her focus. If the church people found out about her therapist, they would have said she lost her faith in God.

Tina opened her heart to her therapist. She started going more in-depth in telling her story. Pastor Henry, her husband, kept his a secret well-hidden. Tina found out by accident. His problem keeps him from sleeping and consumes him day and night. She pretends not to notice the movies on his personal computer. Henry is addicted to porn. *How do I get him back from those women he loves more than me? How do I compete with them? Does he realize he is cheating on me, breaking my heart? The proof of his infidelity peeps its ugly head every time I use his personal computer. Pastor forgets to delete the filth; the ugliness of what he was doing shows up. How does a woman who loves her husband survive in a celibate marriage?*

First Lady Tina lives with a secret she cannot trust with anyone. Her husband is a bishop of several churches all over the country. Can she tell them that her husband does not sleep with her, that he sleeps with his computer in his arms night after night?

Tina tries to look at the porn movies. Maybe we can enjoy them together. She wants to understand the obsession with strange women and men. When she looked at the images, she becomes sick to her stomach. Lord, help me. I do not want to think of my husband as a dirty person. Yet every time I look at him, I see the men and women he is having sex with on the movies. She cannot erase the images from her mind; it is taking her sleep away.

The therapy helps Tina put things into perspective. The great bishop husband is the one with the problem. God is helping Lady Tina keep a sound mind with peace. God is teaching her to lean and depend on Him. *If it were not for me working on myself and understanding my worth, I would have lost my mind or left him.*

Year after year passes The Bishop refused to get help for his addiction. "Tina wonders if her husband will ever change. She worked on herself in therapy, Tina was getting stronger. She prayed that the Lord use her for His glory. Tine understood that it was not her responsibility to improve her husband. She prayed God work on me, *as I pray for my Henry. Tina wanted to see her husband like the Lord saw him. A great man of God that helps people to survive their troubles.* She began a ministry helping other women to cope with challenges in their marriage to a pastor. She held seminars. Many women have talked with her in secret as well. She found a way to help others without exposing her husband.

Tina was happy with herself at last. She no longer worried about her husband's addiction. She was thriving in her personal life. Tina was able to start a nonprofit for women in domestic abuse. She did not divorce her husband; she continued to love him. She enjoyed the parts of him he shared with her. Pastor Henry is a great man and husband tina always exclaimed.

Tina's coping list:

Love bears all things
Love believes all things
Hopes all things
Endures All Things
(1 Corinthians 13:7 NIV)
Pray
Understand

STORY NUMBER SIX
Dating while married

Thirty-two-year-old Pastor Johnny Richards, a handsome six foot four, shows off a chiseled body. He was known for dressing in tailor-made suits every day of the week. The ladies described him having a good sense of humor. His sharp piercing eyes were undressing the Sisters of the Church when he talked with them. The way he looked at the ladies made them blush with excitement. There was always a long line of ladies, single and married, waiting to talk with him at the end of church service. They all wanted their few minutes with the pastor, as they received their unique smile.

He loved smiling with his pearly white teeth, showing off his sharp features. The women talked about his dimples and cheeks with those beautiful full dark lips. Those lips of his are shining with lip balm. He targets women with low self-esteem, the women who were divorced, or lonely married women who needed extra attention from a man.

The pastor took good care of himself, going to the gym five days a week. He loved showing off his well-built body and balanced weight. When he preached, the women became intoxicated.

When he spoke, he had a way of mesmerizing the people.

Pastor Richards married one of the ladies in the church, Latonya Smith, a cute thirty-year-old. Latonya was thirty pounds overweight. She did not have time to go to the gym with her husband. She had the body of a woman who had given birth to three children. Latonya was ashamed of her extended stomach and broad hips.

First Lady Latonya was a teacher by trade, working for the public school system full time. She was shy, stayed to herself, not an outgoing person. She was not a confident woman. She depended on her husband to tell her who she was. She did not do anything without first consulting him. She did not use her voice in church or at home. She was a good mother. She dressed in modest apparel.

They had three children together. Lived in a small town in a lovely three-bedroom house that was in Latonya's name. The pastor's credit was not in good standing. Yet he spent money on jewelry and electronics, using credit cards without paying the bills. The church paid Pastor Richards a salary of $50,000 a year. They purchased him a Cadillac Seville. That was a good salary considering he lived in a small town where the average wage was $35,000 a year. He walked around the small town like a prince wearing his fitted suits.

The townspeople talked about his reputation of dating women and leaving his wife home to tend to the children. People complained he was taking advantage of the church by using the money driving single women around in his Cadillac.

People watched the pastor leave his house late at night to visit with other women of his church. People saw him coming and going form from the local hotel. While in the pulpit, he still did not refrain from saying inappropriate things about women's clothing. He did not discriminate; he made advances toward the married and single women, the young and old. He had no regard for his wife's feelings. It was as if he did not see her sitting in the front listening to him.

Not only did the First Lady have to deal with her husband's disrespect, there was also a female elder named Sandy in the church who did not mind insulting the First Lady. She referred to the pastor as her "church husband." Elder Sandy was married; her husband attended the church. Elder told the First Lady, "If I were not married, he would be mine."

The women treated the First Lady with disrespect. Asked her insulting questions such as, "How do you deal with a powerful man like that? If he were mine, he would get a good meal every night." She was unhappy, yet she did not speak a word. She thought if she prayed and took care of him, he would change and be satisfied with her.

First Lady Latonya tried to talk with her husband/ Pastor concerning his inappropriate flirting with the women in the church. She explained how the women in the church felt it was ok for them to be disrespectful, and how it was hurtful to her. He dismissed her with "They are my members."

Pastor Richards was preaching the Sunday morning a beautiful petite woman walked through the doors wearing a mini skirt and a tight pink sweater exposing her bosom. She walked to the front of the church sat down, crossed her legs showing her thighs. She waited until the church service was over and told the pastor she needed counseling. He said yes, of course. He told his wife he was counseling a new member of the church. Latonya asks if she could go with him, "No, it's a private meeting. She does not want anyone except for me to hear her business."

After that initial meeting, Pastor and the pink blouse continued meeting outside of the church at least three times a week. The woman's behavior became brazen. It was apparent to everyone that she was setting herself up to be the next first lady.

Sure enough, the pastor left his wife and three children for Sister pink blouse. He went home one day, pack his bags and left. He explained to the church members that his wife left him; she no longer wanted to be his wife or a first lady. He paid her to leave without a fight. He allowed her to sell the house and move out of town. No one ever heard from her again.

The church members accepted the story. It was church as usual. The new wife took her seat in the front. They purchased a home. She was soon pregnant. Together they had three children. Someone said three was the pastor's magic number when it came to children, and who knows, maybe marriages as well.

After seven years with First Lady pink blouse he began to be discontent and look around for another woman. He loved the women in the church; the pastor felt they belonged to him. He began to smile at his church secretary Stephanie. She knew what he wanted; she smiled back. Pastor Richards went into her office one day after service to see how much money was collected. Stephanie took off her dress and supplied his need. He fell for the secretary. Once again, he started dating while married. After six months, the secretary informed the pastor that she cannot commit adultery any more. Stephanie wanted marriage. Pastor Richards did

not hesitate to send divorce papers to the wife's job. Lady pink blouse was shocked. The same

way First Lady pink blouse schemed to cheat with the pastor, the church secretary took Pastor Johnny Richards from her.

"Do not deceived: God cannot be mocked. A man reaps what he sows, Whoever sows to please their flesh, from the flesh will reap destruction whoever sows to please the spirit, from the spirit will reap eternal life. everlasting." (Galatians 6:7-9 NIV)

STORY NUMBER SEVEN
District Lady Samantha

District Elect First Lady Samantha King was the most powerful woman in her Church. **I Believe in God, Church of Holiness.** Supervised thirty churches and born of modest means, her parents were teachers and raised Samantha to be intelligent and confident in her abilities no matter what she chooses to do with her life. They sent her to a women's college in Atlanta.

Bishop Jonathan King was in college, walking down the street. His eyes glanced a beautiful young girl walking toward him, and he said hello. She did not acknowledge. He kept moving. The next day, he saw her again. Jonathan tried to get her attention, no luck. He had to do something. Samantha intrigued him. Jonathan walked the same way back the next day. Jonathan decided that he was going to take her out and she was going to be his wife. He continued to walk the same route the same time every day. When she said hello that was his opening.

He asked her if he could take her out for pizza, and she said yes. During the conversation, he mentioned that after he graduated from college, he had a church waiting for him to lead. She nodded her head impressed. Johnathan asks her if she knew the Lord. She said, "No, I am not religious. I do not know anything about God. I have no time for church or God."

They continued to date. Bishop King proposed to Samantha after they graduated college. She laughed, "I am not marrying a pastor. I do not know what a pastor does." As time continued, he did not stop seeing her. Jonathan invited her to church every week. She said no every time. One day he looked up, and Samantha was in the church. She watched him preach and was impressed. She looked around at the people and their reaction to him. She decided at that point that he was awesome. She took him serious about Jesus. She received Jesus as her Lord and Savior.

The pastor tried again for her hand in marriage; this time, she said yes. They had two children, and the Church increased in numbers. She served as the District Elect First Lady Samantha King. The women often sized her up, checking to find out if she had what was needed to be the First Lady. She became well-known as a soft-spoken woman who carried a big stick. She is was proving to be perfect for her title of Elect First Lady. She accepted no disrespect from anyone. She used the word of God to protect herself and others. "Show proper respect to everyone, love the family of believers, fear God, and honor the emperor." (1 Peter 2:17 NIV)

Lady Samantha did not consider herself a preacher had no desire to preach. Leaders from other churches requested her to speak to their women. They believed her to be a great example of excellence and success as a first lady married to a pastor. "I will speak to the women on how to care for their family and be their true self."

Her main objective was to take care of her husband, making sure he was happy to do his job as District Bishop. He had a great responsibility supervising one of the largest churches in Atlanta. She took care of her home and children.

If there was ever a woman filled with confidence and strength, it was Lady Samantha. When most first ladies walked into a room, the first thing noticed was their beautiful designer clothing, fine jewelry, and the big colorful rhinestone hat with the purse to match.

When Lady Elect Samantha walked into the sanctuary, all noticed her three-inch heels, and her signature rhinestones on her shoes. She had what the other first ladies had: elegant suits, shoes, hats, and purses. Lady Samantha's attire did not define her. Beautiful attire is part of the perks of marrying a rich man. When she walked into the sanctuary, she radiated confidence, head held high.

All the district First Ladies had assigned seats during the yearly District Conference. They were seated front stage on the pulpit for all to see them. The First Ladies walked into the sanctuary together as they took their seats. Music played, the announcement made for everyone to acknowledge the ladies. Each lady received a place showing off their femininity.

After the District Ladies took their seats. The announcement was made for the bishop's wife to enter, "Please let us all stand as Lady Elect Samantha enters the sanctuary." One would think they were standing for royalty, The Pope, or the President of the United States. It was quite a performance.

As all stopped and watched Lady Samantha glide into the room, Elect Lady Samantha enters, exuding confidence.

District Lady Samantha

She takes her time as she waves at the people before taking her assigned seat in front of the other women.

Her husband takes his place at the mic to speak. "Please clap for my beautiful wife, the Elect Lady of this District." The hand-clapping goes on for five minutes. The women were in awe, looking at the four foot nine tiny goddesses.

She was a prize to her husband, and she knew it. Samantha did not concern herself with jealousy over other women attracted to her husband. She was as feminine as any woman. She was not concerned about the other women desiring her man, and they did.

Lady Elect Samantha was wanted by men just as much as women wanted him. She was favorable in her ability to be herself, and she walked in her authority. She did not work an outside job; Samantha did not want for anything. Samantha held a bachelor's degree in education. The bishop took care of her. The mansion with a home theater, furs, jewelry. She was worth it all to him. She never reminded him that she was worth it all; he proved it to her. Church people behind her back called her First Lady Everything.

She was everything to her husband, and he was everything to her. Oh, the women called him handsome. He wore a suit like no man should wear a suit. His suits fit him like he was born into them. When the two of them walked into a room together, they were the perfect power couple. All one felt was the power to match their humble spirits.

They were like thunder and lightning, altogether powerful. When the bishop introduced his wife, his face lit up. He had the sweetest way of saying, "Come here, babe." She'd smile, glide up to him, give a hug, and go back to her assigned seat, crossing her legs and waiting for him to speak.

They were a great example of leadership. Bishop King and Lady Samantha treated people with love and respect. The First Ladies of the District looked up to her even though she was younger than most of them. People said that God had shown Samantha favor. It was clear to all who knew Elect Lady Samantha King that she was doing what she was called to do.

She is the First Lady of a black Church.

CONCLUSION

You desire to be a Pastor's Wife. All that glitters is not gold. And all that is dull may shine bright for you. Do not look at the outward appearance only. Pray long and hard; hear the voice of the Lord. Maybe you can handle what you hear and perhaps you cannot.

Look into the background and the character of the person. Maybe you were chosen to be with that man. It takes a special anointing to be with a pastor.

Whether you agree with me or not, pray for the First Lady you know. She needs your earnest prayers.

In the church setting, we look at the Pastor and his relationship with his wife. If he is not treating her well, half of the woman say I do not want to marry a pastor. The other half who think being a pastor's wife is the glamorous dream.

Beware you who believe the Pastor is your Prince Charming. Some have found out that he is toxic at home. A pastor is a man full of flaws and greatness.

Time over for the passive First Lady of the Church that is not talking. God has given us a voice to use for his glory. No longer is anyone to treat you like a person to be trampled on. You are warriors put on the whole Armour on God. (Ephesians 6:13 NIV) Dress for the position. The weapons we fight with are not the weapons of the world. On the contrary, they have divine power to demolish arguments and every pretension that sets itself up against the knowledge of God, and we take captive every thought to make it obedient to Christ. Ladies unite together to get out of the closet of shame. Use other first ladies as your confidants. Team up together for prayer.

People not on your side may become upset because you use your voice. Use your full voice; some will be able to handle your voice it and some will not. Speak up and judge fairly; defend the right of the poor and needy. (Proverbs 31:8)

Testimony: As for me, I had to go through much pain to get the courage to use my voice. It was not a full expression of who I was. Some members of the church devised a vicious plan to chase me away. People allow the enemy to trick them into the deceitful practice of jealously and hate. They missed the fact that God put me in that position of the first lady. They lost their blessing. I wanted to help them build the ministry. I saw them as a family; they saw me as a threat to what they had in place. I desired to become a part of the Christian family. What then, shall we say to these thing If God is for us who can be against us? (Romans 8:31 NIV)

"If anyone will not welcome you, or listen to your words, leave that home or town and shake the dust off your feet. " (Matthew 10:14 NIV)

LESSON: THE GREEN GRASS

*B*e careful looking at the landscape on someone else's lawn. It may be green, tall, and beautiful in color. Looking at the grass of others will tempt you want to go to where the beauty is. Do not allow the enemy of your mind to deceive you into touching, smelling, or looking at something that does not belong to you. The hard work was done behind the scenes. You cannot see the toll they put into it by looking from afar. Maybe they hired someone to keep it. Possibly the owners worked on it themselves. The grass does not belong to you. You can get in much trouble looking at what belongs to someone else and covet what they have.

You shall not covet thy neighbor's house. You shalt not covet your neighbors' wife, or his male or his female servant, his ox, or donkey, or anything that belongs to his neighbor.

(Exodus 20:17 NIV) in other words if it is not yours leave it alone.

Do not covet a person's position; God has given you your gift and vision for your life. When you want someone's place, you miss the blessing designed for you.

Look what happened to David. David was not where he was supposed to be. We can also say that his mind was not in the right place.

In the spring, at the time when kings go off to war, David sent Joab out with the King's men and the whole

Israelite army. They destroyed the Ammonites and besieged Rabbah. But David remained in Jerusalem. (2 Samuel 11:1 NIV)

One evening David got up from his bed and walked around on the roof of the palace. From the roof, he saw a woman bathing. The woman was incredibly beautiful, and David sent someone to find out about her. The man said, "She is Bathsheba, the daughter of Eliam and the wife of Uriah the Hittite." 4 Then David sent messengers to get her. She came to him, and he slept with her. (Now she was purifying herself from her monthly uncleanness.) Then she went back home. 5 The woman conceived and sent word to David, saying, "I am pregnant." (2 Samuel 11:5 NIV)

When King David committed adultery with Bathsheba, he tried to cover up her pregnancy, and when he failed with that, he had her husband Uriah the Hittite killed. That was perhaps the most significant transgression of David's life.

When we covet, we transgress against God that person or thing we are wanting. That desire can stop and prolong what God intends for us and set the trajectory for us going in the wrong direction. What is for you is for you if you live right. Trust the Lord to lead and guide you. It may seem like things are taking too long but wait on the Lord. It would be in your best interest. Make the right decisions and prosper.

Pray before your leap. Ask the Lord which way to go. Just because it looks good does not mean it is right for you. Because you can do something, it does not say it is the best thing to do. When we make a mistake (it is ok we all make them), do not give up; pray and live another day. If we sin repent. God is a forgiving God.

God bless you

MEET THE AUTHOR
Lorraine Jenkins Wilkes

I am a Brooklyn-born minister based in North Carolina. Talk about culture shock. It took years to adjust to the change in pace and the constant greeting on the street, but I have learned to love my new life thanks to my southern-born husband and my church.

I have always believed in the healing power of laughter, used in tough life situations. I have worked in the health care field for over thirty years. Chaplain for a large healthcare organization, Master Storyteller, speaker, a Certified Assisted Living Administrator, and a Certified Life Recovery Coach. I hold a bachelor's degree in Theology and two associates degrees in healthcare. visionary of a Christian talk show called the Power of S.H.E., I published my memoir *Forever Home*, as well as *Courage to Change* and *Courage to Change: Devotional Journal*, Rising with the Son Day by Day.

I do not beat around the bush, finding Jesus is the number one factor during my life. As a child, I was left to fend for myself and four younger sisters on the streets of New York. Later, we were placed in the care of a relative, and the abuse ensued. As abuse and degradation became familiar, I unknowingly created this pattern in my relationships. As a young child, I learned that I was of low value; through Christ, I learned I was precious and carefully made.

My calling in life came at the cost of living the trauma of rejection and domestic abuse, along with witnessing my mother institutionalized at an early age. My vision is to help those stuck in their past hurts, to survive and thrive with the help of the Lord Jesus Christ. I am saved, Love the Lord Jesus Christ. I want to see people whole in every area of their life.

Moto take care of the entire person, change your life change your future.

Booking information:
Lorrainejenkins-wilkes.com
Email: powerofshe123@gmail.com
Facebook
10% of proceeds will be donated to benefits those suffering from domestic abuse

Other books
Forever Home

Lorraine Jenkins Wilkes

Courage to Change
Courage to Change Devotional/Journal
Rising with the Son, Day by Day

www.ingramcontent.com/pod-product-compliance
Lightning Source LLC
Chambersburg PA
CBHW031208090426
42736CB00009B/836